Wild Cats of the World Coloring Book

by John Green

Introduction and Captions by Stig Asplund

DOVER PUBLICATIONS, INC.

New York

Copyright

Copyright © 1988 by John Green
All rights reserved.

Bibliographical Note

Wild Cats of the World Coloring Book is a new work, first published by Dover Publications, Inc., in 1988.

International Standard Book Number
ISBN-13: 978-0-486-25638-2
ISBN-10: 0-486-25638-3

Manufactured in the United States by Courier Corporation
25638315   2013
www.doverpublications.com

Introduction

Felines, the members of the cat family (Felidae), belong to the order of flesh-eating mammals (Carnivora). The domestic cat (*Felis catus*) is, of course, in this family, and all the wild members—despite differences in size, proportions and coloration—bear an unmistakable resemblance to that universally familiar animal. All are muscular and lithe, with a round head and with sharp teeth and claws; all are hunters of prey; all are wary and aloof.

The present volume illustrates and briefly describes every living wild feline species, with the single exception of the little-known Iriomote cat (*Felis iriomotensis*), found only on the island of that name close to Taiwan.

Among the biologists who classify felines on the basis of anatomy and other factors, there is still much controversy over the subdivision of the family into genera.[1] For example, some authorities recognize only the two genera *Felis* and *Acinonyx*; others use the genus name *Leo* instead of *Panthera*; etc. The present book uses the classification adopted in the standard reference work *Walker's Mammals of the World* (4th edition, 2 volumes), edited by Ronald M. Nowak and John L. Paradiso, published by The Johns Hopkins University Press, Baltimore, 1983. *Walker's* is followed here both for the scientific name (in Latin) of each cat and for the exact form of its principal common name (in English)—except that "puma" and rather than "cougar" has been chosen here as the principal common name of *Felis concolor*.[2]

Only one scientific name, the *Walker's* version, is given in the present captions, but alternate common names are supplied wherever known. Alphabetical lists of scientific names and of alternate common names will be found overleaf. The main part of the book is arranged alphabetically by the principal common names.

In addition to nomenclature, the captions contain the following information as known or applicable: coloration (for further guidance on coloring of the cats, see the colored renderings of many of them on the covers of the book); dimensions (the dimensions given are always those of the largest adult males in the species; the length given is that of the head plus body, minus the tail; the height given is that to the shoulder); habitat and geographic distribution; habits, prey and other relevant facts; rarity and/or endangered status; alternate common names.

[1]Genera (singular: genus) are subgroups below family (and subfamily) level. A genus usually includes several species (the next lower subgroup), but sometimes only one; for instance, the genus *Acinonyx* includes the single species *Acinonyx jubatus* (cheetah), and the genus *Neofelis* includes the single species *Neofelis nebulosa* (clouded leopard). Many species also include subspecies indicated by the addition of a third Latin word, as in *Panthera tigris sumatrae*, the Sumatran tiger, a subspecies of the tiger (*Panthera tigris*).

[2]*Walker's*, though not the only source of statistics for the captions in the present book, has nevertheless been indispensable, especially for the rare animals not described in any other readily accessible work.

ALPHABETICAL LIST OF SCIENTIFIC NAMES

ALPHABETICAL LIST OF ALTERNATE COMMON NAMES

African golden cat (*Felis aurata*). COLORATION: Brownish or grayish fur, white underparts; brown or gray spots all over, or just on belly and the inside of the legs. Length 40″, height 15″, weight 35 lb. Lives in forested parts of Africa south of the Sahara. Active day or night, a solitary hunter of birds and small hoofed mammals. Also known as West African golden cat.

5

Asian golden cat (*Felis temmincki*). COLORATION: Individuals range from golden red to gray; white and black facial streaks; some specimens are spotted. Length 40″, weight 33 lb. Lives in forests from Tibet through India into the Malay Peninsula and Sumatra. It hunts in pairs, feeding on small mammals, birds and lizards. Endangered. Also known as Eastern golden cat.

Bay cat (*Felis badia*). COLORATION: Chestnut, with pale belly; white tail tip. Length 24″. Lives in dense forests in Borneo. Vary rare; its habits not yet thoroughly studied.

Black-footed cat (*Felis nigripes*). COLORATION: Ochre (its back darker than its belly); dark spots on body; two dark streaks on each cheek; bars on legs, haunches and tail; black tip to tail; bottom of feet black. Length 20″, weight 6 lb. Lives in dry, open country in southern Africa. Solitary night hunter of rodents, birds and reptiles.

Bobcat (*Felis rufus*). COLORATION: Buff to brown; underparts white; dark spots and lines; backs of ears marked with black; black tip on upper side of tail. Small ear tufts; ruff on jowls. Length 40″, height 23″, weight 34 lb. Lives in a wide variety of habitats from southern Canada to central Mexico. Stalks small mammals and birds, sometimes deer, at night. Solitary, silent; highly territorial habits (marking, patrolling and defending a fixed area). Under government protection. Also known as bay lynx and wildcat.

9

Caracal (*Felis caracal*). COLORATION: Reddish brown; chin, throat and belly white; black lines on forehead; ears black with long black tufts. Length 36″, height 20″, weight 42 lb. Lives in dry areas (but not deserts) in most of Africa and southwest Asia from Arabia to India. Fastest feline of its size range. Stalks birds, rodents and small antelopes at night. Has been tamed for hunting in Iran and India. Scarce in some areas. Also known as Persian lynx and desert lynx.

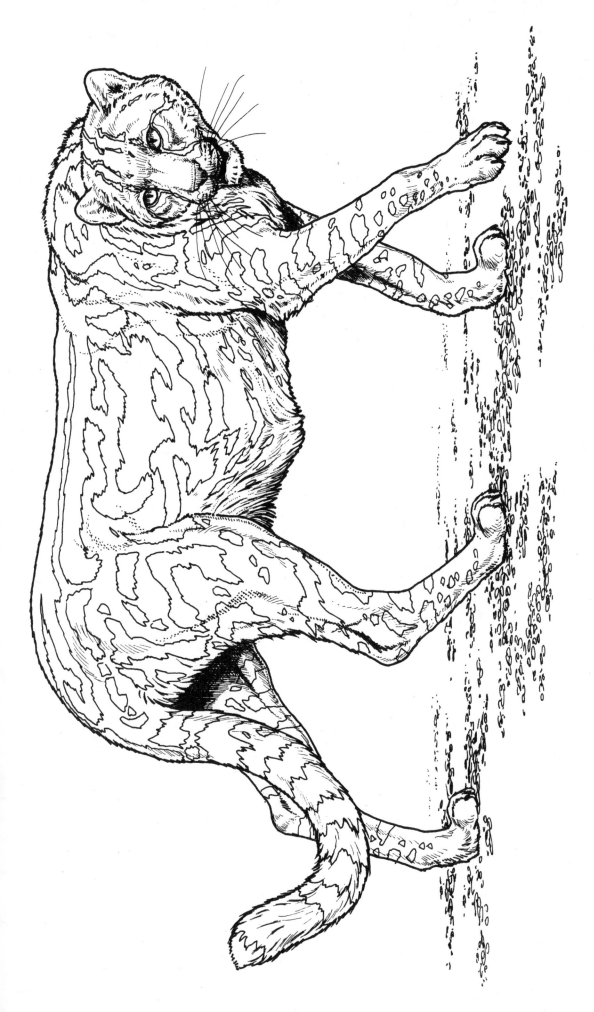

Cheetah (*Acinonyx jubatus*). COLORATION: Tawny to grayish, paler below; black stripe from eye to mouth; most often with round black spots (as on pages 12 and 13); the very rare barred specimens, like the one on this page, were once considered a separate species, known as the king cheetah. Length 60″, height 36″, weight 160 lb. Lives in habitats varying from semidesert to thick bush in Africa (everywhere except tropical forests and central Sahara) and in Asia from the Mediterranean to Central India. (*More about cheetahs overleaf.*)

11

Cheetah (continued). Cheetahs are daytime hunters, sprinting after their prey (small hoofed mammals) in spurts of up to 70 miles per hour—making them the swiftest of land mammals. They have been tamed for hunting for millennia in various Asian cultures. Their claws cannot be fully retracted. Adversely affected by the proximity of man, their numbers are dwindling and approaching the endangered level. Also known as hunting leopard.

Chinese desert cat (*Felis bieti*). COLORATION: Yellowish gray, darker on the back; black rings and tip on tail. Length 33″. Lives in steppes and lightly wooded mountain areas of southern Mongolia and central China. Habits not yet sufficiently investigated.

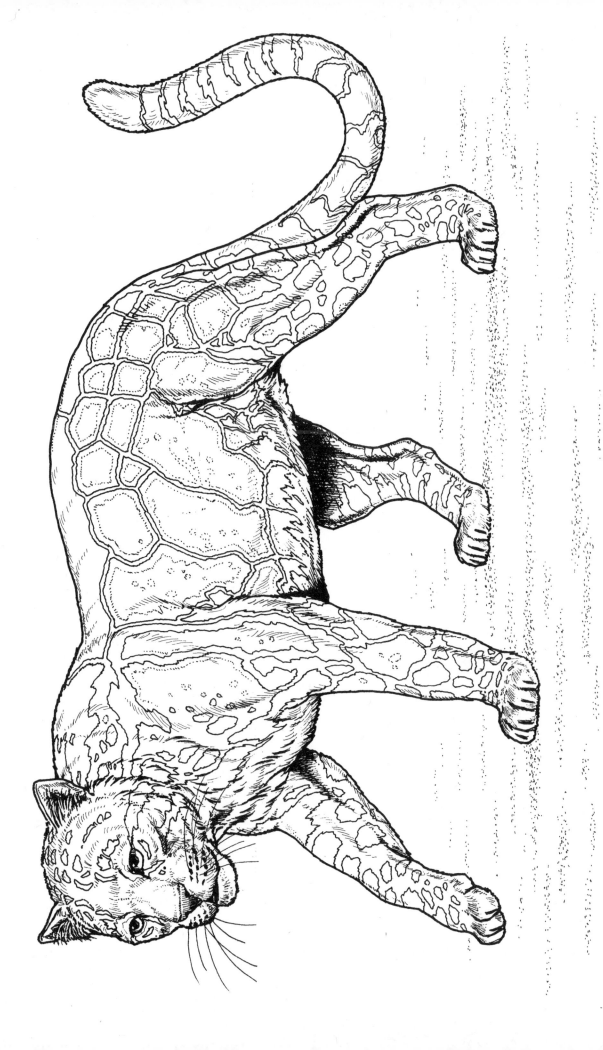

Clouded leopard (*Neofelis nebulosa*). COLORATION: Grayish or yellowish; black-edged dark markings of irregular shape. Length 42″, height 32″, weight 50 lb. Lives in forests in Southeast Asia and Indonesia from Nepal to Borneo. Unusually long canine teeth; has the ability to roar. Tree-dweller; eats a variety of small animals; is itself hunted by man (endangered). Also known as clouded tiger.

Fishing cat (*Felis viverrinus*). COLORATION: Grayish or brownish; dark brown spots; dark lines on forehead. Claws cannot be completely retracted; some webbing between toes of forefeet. Length 34″, height 16″, weight 30 lb. Lives in thickets and swamps from Pakistan to Southeast Asia and parts of Indonesia. Eats fish (which it scoops up) and other small creatures. Wades and swims well.

Flat-headed cat (*Felis planiceps*). COLORATION: Dark brown with a silvery tinge; underparts white with brown splashes; top of head reddish brown. Claws cannot be completely retracted. Length 20″, weight 5 lb. Lives in Malaya, Sumatra and Borneo. Active at night; eats frogs and fish. Extremely rare.

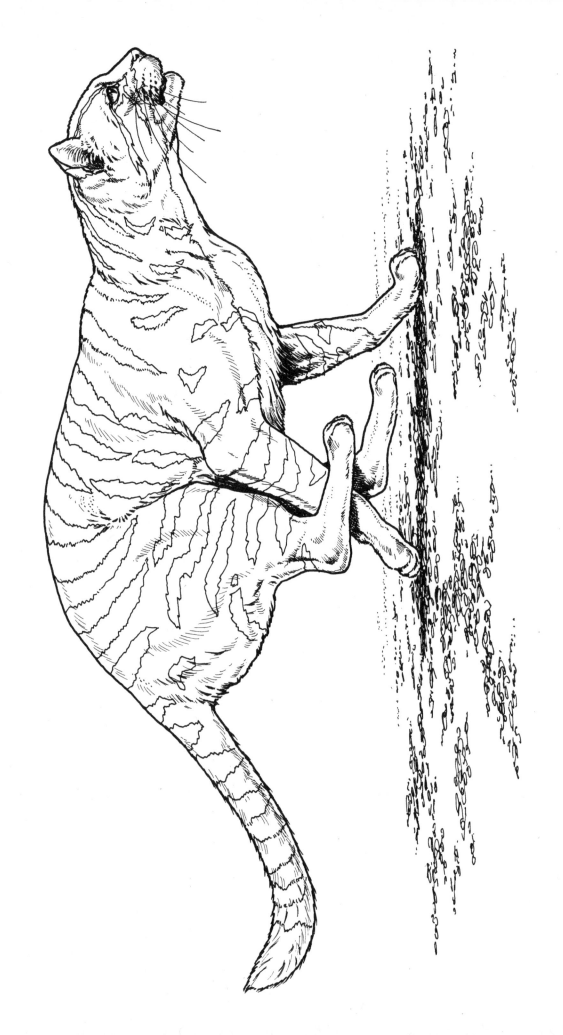

Geoffroy's cat (*Felis geoffroyi*). COLORATION: Wide color range from ochre to gray; small black spots and streaks; ringed tail. Length 28″. Lives in scrub and bush country in South America from Bolivia to Patagonia, occurring even in high mountain areas. Good swimmer. Eats small mammals and birds.

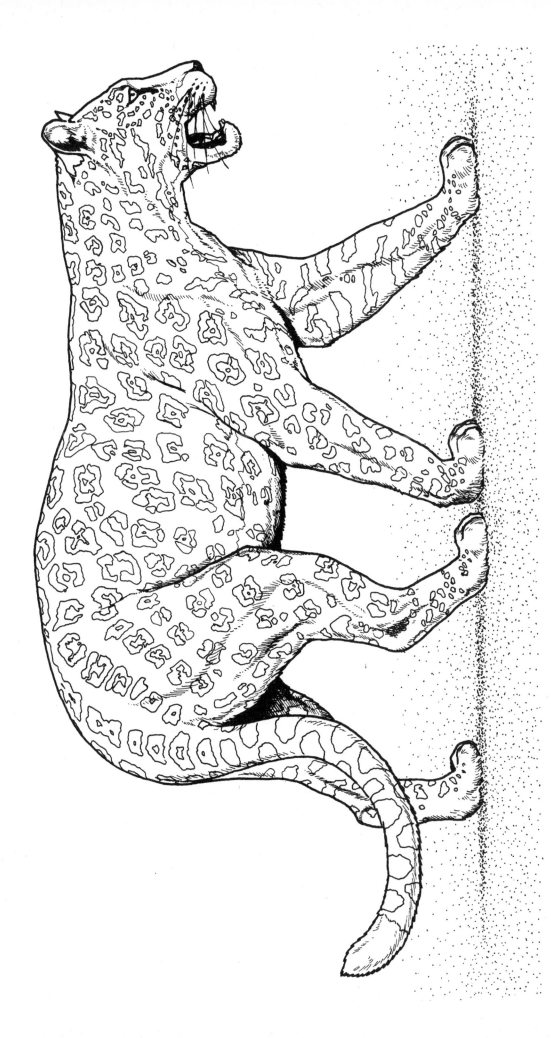

Jaguar (*Panthera onca*). COLORATION: Basic color varies between yellow and reddish-brown; paler below; black spots and rosettes. Length 70″, height 30″, weight 350 lb. Largest New World feline (and the only one able to roar), it lives in a wide variety of habitats (forest, grassland, even desert) from the southern U.S. to Argentina. Often in trees, it hunts on the ground at night for rodents and hoofed mammals. Human inroads on its territory, as well as killings for fur, have brought it close to the endangered status.

Jaguarundi (*Felis yagouaroundi*). COLORATION: Grayish or reddish. Length 30″, height 12″, weight 20 lb. Lives in lowland forests and thickets from southwestern U.S. to northern Argentina. Active day and night, it hunts birds and small mammals. Some subspecies are endangered. Also known as otter-cat and (when reddish) as eyra.

Jungle cat (*Felis chaus*). COLORATION: From yellow-gray to gray-brown or tawny; tail has dark tip and rings. Length 30″, weight 35 lb. Lives in forests or open areas, including mountains, in Egypt, Russia and across southern Asia to China and Southeast Asia. Birds, small mammals and other little animals are hunted by the jungle cat by day or by night.

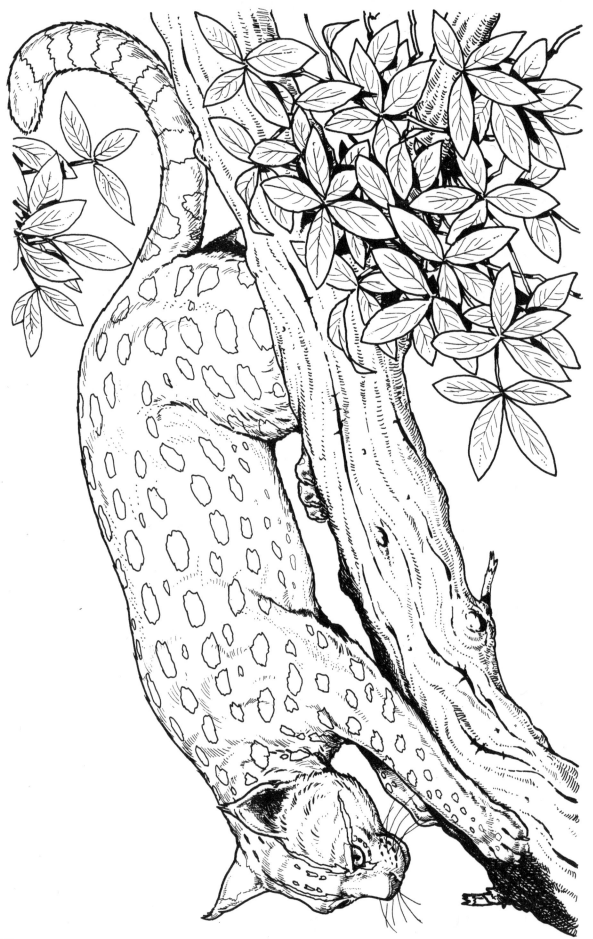

Kodkod (*Felis guigna*). COLORATION: Buff to brown, with dark spots and rings on tail. Length 19″. Lives in forests in parts of Chile and Argentina. Active at night. Eats small mammals. Some observers state that it spends most of its time in trees.

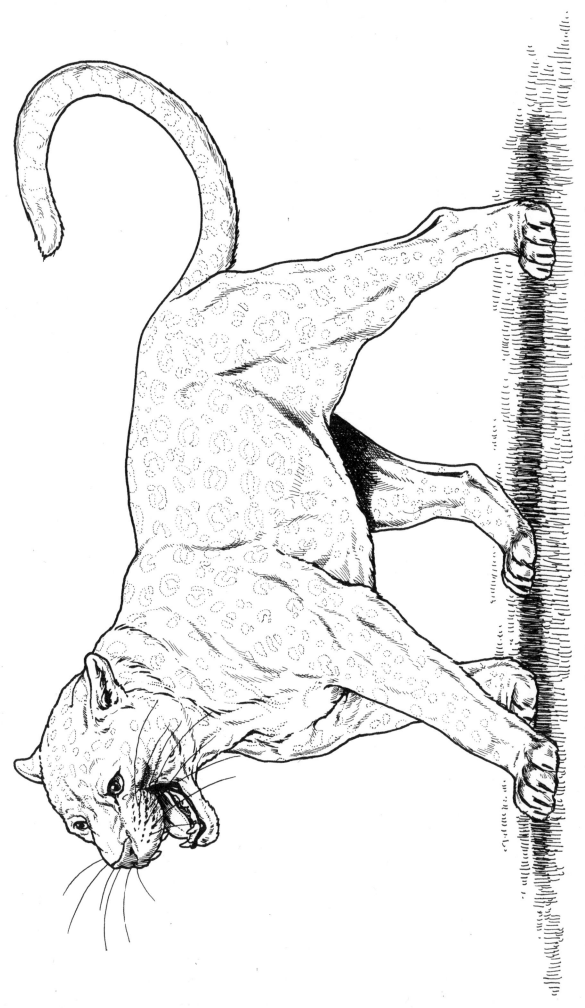

Leopard (*Panthera pardus*). COLORATION: Most specimens are buff to chestnut, with white underparts and a dense pattern of spots and rosettes (this type, also known as panther, is illustrated on the next page). The leopard on this page is one of the melanistic specimens (black all over, but with the spots visible) not uncommon in the moist forest areas of the leopard's range; this type is also known as black panther. (Melanism also occurs in other feline species, but not so commonly.) Length 70″, height 30″, weight 200 lb. (*More about leopards overleaf.*)

Leopard (continued). Lives in almost any habitat in Africa south of the Sahara and the southern half of Asia. Stalks hoofed mammals, monkeys and other smaller animals at night, resting by day usually in trees, where it also stores unconsumed prey. One of the big roaring cats. Usually solitary; highly territorial habits; sometimes attacks man. Sought for its fur, it is becoming rare in North Africa and in Asia; some subspecies endangered.

Leopard cat (*Felis bengalensis*). COLORATION: Light tawny, white below; dark spots; bands on forehead; tail ends in rings. Length 42″, weight 15 lb. Lives in highland and lowland forests in the eastern band of Asia from southeastern Siberia to Indonesia. Its den is in a hollow tree or small cave; it hunts many small animals, chiefly at night. Swims well.

Lion (*Panthera leo*). COLORATION: Buff to brown (some are gray), with paler underparts; black tail tuft; mane (in males) can range from yellow to black. Length 100″, height 48″, weight 550 lb. Found at present in Africa south of the Sahara (the illustration on this page shows a typical African specimen) and in a small enclave in India (the illustration on the next page shows the Indian subspecies *Panthera leo persica*, which is endangered). In historic times the lion ranged much more widely (throughout Africa and from southeastern Europe through to India); in prehistory it had the greatest range worldwide of any wild land mammal. (*More about lions on facing page.*)

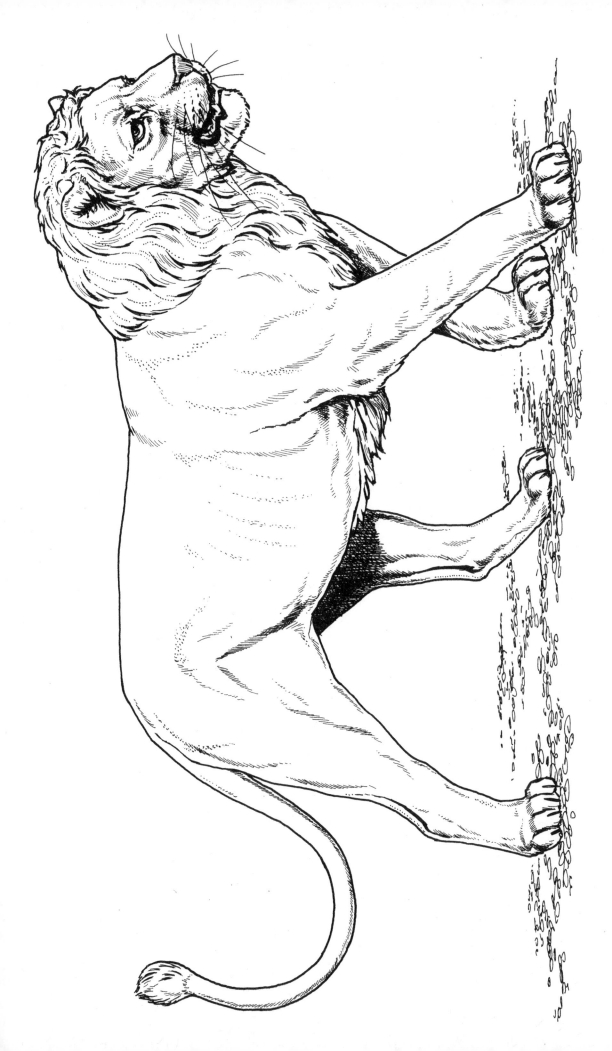

Lion (continued). Found in a single forest in India, it occurs in Africa chiefly on grassy plains and in open woods, though it may occupy almost any terrain, even very high mountains. It hunts chiefly at night or at dusk, alone, in pairs or in groups, seeking hoofed mammals such as zebras and antelopes but also eating carrion. It may spend up to 21 hours of each day in repose. One of the big roaring cats. The social groups of lions, known as prides, are composed of related females and their young, to which males attach themselves. Some lions are migratory.

27

Little spotted cat (*Felis tigrinus*). COLORATION: Ochre, paler below; dark spots; tail with rings and black tip. Length 22″, weight 6 lb. Lives in forests in Central and South America from Costa Rica to Argentina. Hunted for its fur; endangered. Also known as tiger cat.

Lynx (*Felis lynx*). COLORATION: From buff to gray (some can be spotted); black tail tip; long black ear tufts. Long fur on jowls. Length 48″, height 30″, weight 80 lb. Lives in forests or tundra in Europe, northern Asia, Alaska, Canada and extreme north of U.S. (the Eurasian specimens are larger than the North American). Solitary night hunter of deer, rabbits and other mammals (in Canada, depends on availability of snowshoe rabbits for food, so those two populations fluctuate in direct proportion). Hunted by man as a pest and for its fur. The North American variety, known as Canada lynx, was once considered a separate species.

Marbled cat (*Felis marmorata*). COLORATION: Ranges from gray to yellow to brown; marked with dark blotches rimmed with black; black tail tip. Length 21″, weight 11 lb. Lives in forests in Southeast Asia and parts of Indonesia. Eats birds and small mammals. Habits not fully known; probably active at night. Very rare; probably endangered.

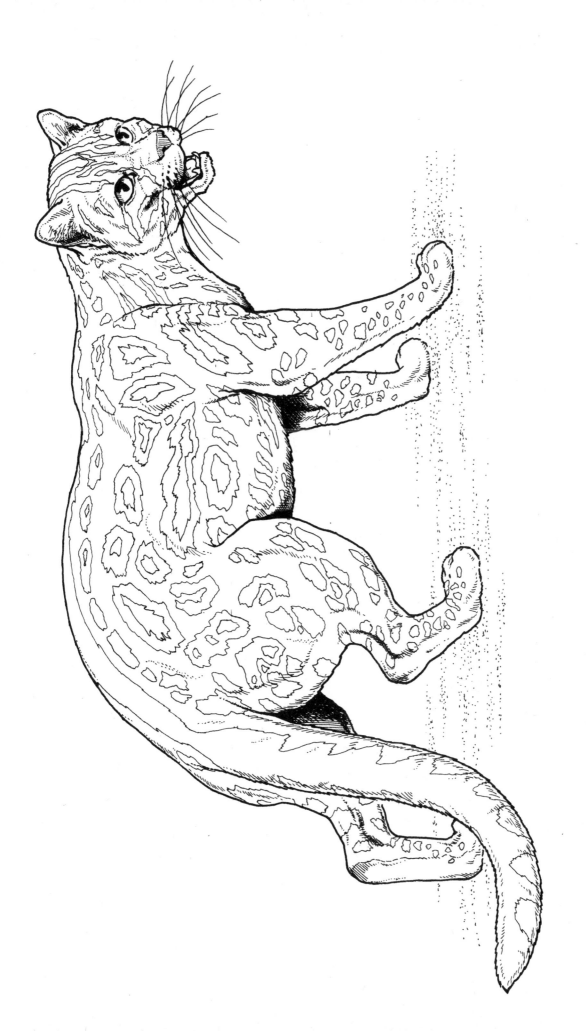

Margay (*Felis wiedii*). COLORATION: Yellowish brown, white below; dark brown spots. Length 32". Lives in trees in forests from Mexico through the northern half of South America. Can be tamed when caught young. Very rare; endangered. Also known as tiger cat and tigrillo.

Mountain cat (*Felis jacobita*). COLORATION: Silvery gray with brown spots and stripes; whitish underparts; tail ringed with a light tip. Length 24″. Lives in high, arid areas of the Andes from southern Peru to northern Chile and Argentina. Eats chinchillas and other small mammals. Rare, perhaps endangered. Also known as Andean mountain cat.

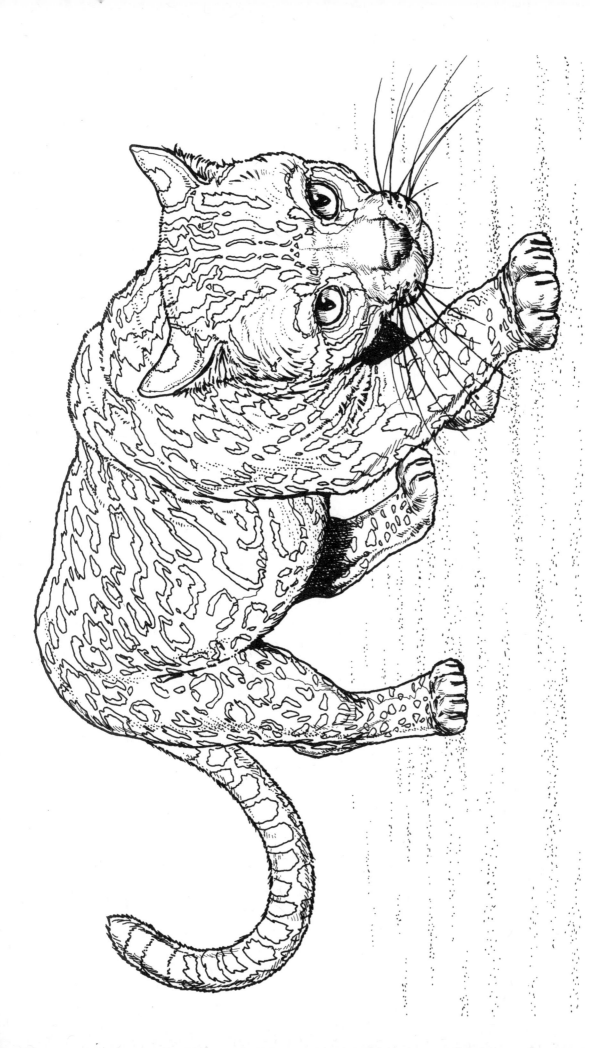

Ocelot (*Felis pardalis*). COLORATION: Whitish, gray or tawny with dark streaks and spots. Length 40″, weight 35 lb. Lives in habitats ranging from moist forests to dry scrub from southwestern U.S. to northern Argentina. Hunts, on the ground at night, small mammals, birds and fish. Often kept as pet; hunted for fur; may be endangered.

Pallas's cat (*Felis manul*). COLORATION: From gray to russet, but hairs have white tips; tail has rings and dark tip. Extremely thick fur on belly protects it from cold. Length 26″, weight 8 lb. Lives in steppes, deserts and rocky and mountainous terrain in Asia from Iran through southeastern Siberia. Spends days in caves or burrows; hunts small mammals at night. Also known as steppe cat and manill.

Pampas cat (*Felis colocolo*). COLORATION: Yellowish, brown or gray, with yellow or brown bands; bars across cheeks. Length 28″, height 14″. Lives in grasslands, forests and mountains in South America from Ecuador to Patagonia. Hunts small mammals at night.

Puma (*Felis concolor*). COLORATION: Either ranging from buff to reddish, or else some shade of gray. Length 75″, weight 225 lb. Lives in almost any wild habitat from western Canada and U.S. in a continuous range to the tip of South America (widest range of any New World mammal). Largest member of genus *Felis* (tropical specimens smaller than those in temperate areas). Active day or night over very large territories. Eats deer and other mammals; has been known to attack people. Now rare in Canada and U.S.; some subspecies endangered. Also known as cougar, mountain lion, panther, American lion, deer tiger, Mexican lion, painter and catamount.

Rusty-spotted cat (*Felis rubiginosus*). COLORATION: Gray with a reddish tinge; white underparts; brown blotches; dark streaks on face and forehead. Length 19″. Lives in grassy or scrubby areas in southern India, and in moist mountain forests in Sri Lanka. Night hunter of birds and small mammals.

Sand cat (*Felis margarita*). COLORATION: Sandy to ochre, with white belly; reddish streak on each cheek; tail has rings and a black tip. Length 23″. Lives in desert areas from Morocco through Central Asia and Pakistan. Its padded soles allow it to walk on sand; it apparently does not need water sources apart from its food, which consists of jerboas and the like, caught at night or at dusk. Rare; at least one subspecies endangered.

Serval (*Felis serval*). COLORATION: From off-white to dark gold, with paler underparts. The type with small dark spots, illustrated on this page, is also known as servaline cat, and used to be considered as a separate species. The type with large spots is illustrated on the following page; these spots merge into stripes. The tail has rings and a black tip. (*More about servals overleaf.*)

Serval (continued). Length 40″, height 25″, weight 40 lb. Lives in grasslands in Morocco, Algeria and the parts of Africa south of the Sahara. A solitary night hunter of birds and mice, it is itself hunted by man for its fur and as a pest. Rare; at least one subspecies endangered.

Snow leopard (*Panthera uncia*). COLORATION: Grayish with whitish underparts; dark spots and rosettes. Length 52″, height 24″, weight 170 lb. Lives in very high mountains of Central Asia. Hunts hoofed mammals and rodents. Studies in the wild of its habits are being actively pursued. Definitely endangered; a multinational system of protection has been instituted. The snow leopard has become a prime symbol of conservationists, along with the panda. Also known as ounce.

Spanish lynx (*Felis pardina*). COLORATION: Upper parts yellow-red, underparts white; round black spots. Has ear tufts and long fur on jowls. Length 42", height 28". Lives in open forests in increasingly diminished areas of Spain and Portugal. Eats rabbits. Endangered.

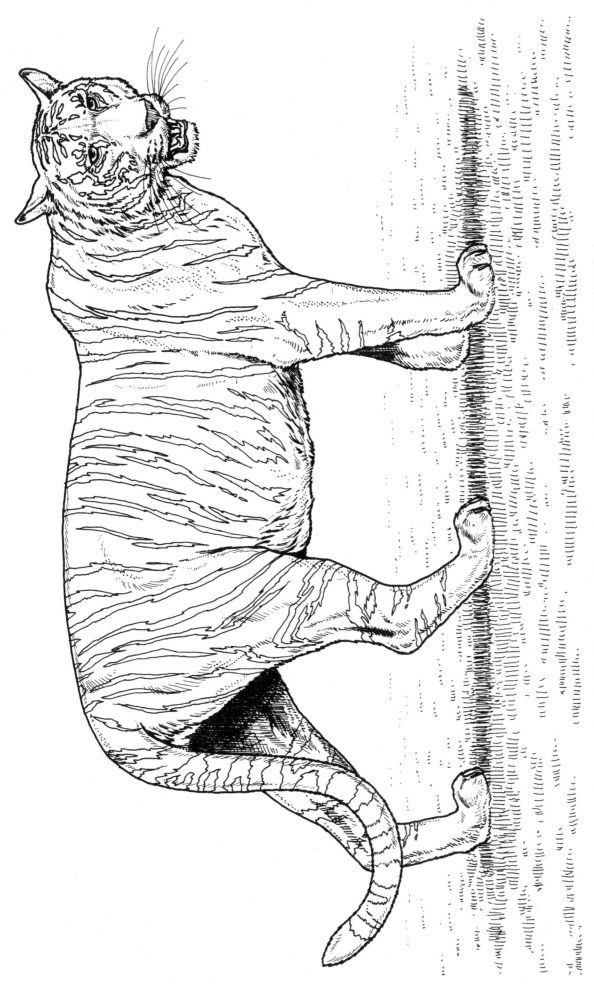

Tiger (*Panthera tigris*). COLORATION: From red-orange to red-ochre; pale or white belly; black, gray or brown stripes. The animal depicted on this page is one of the rare black-and-white tigers that occur in the Rewa district of north-central India. The tigers on the following pages are examples of the brightly colored Sumatra subspecies (*Panthera tigris sumatrae*), which weigh only up to 310 lb. Length of the largest tigers (the Manchurian subspecies) 110", weight 670 lb. (*More about tigers overleaf.*)

Tiger (continued). One of the large roaring cats. Lives in forests and grasslands in the eastern half of Asia from southeastern Siberia through India and Indonesia. Solitary night hunter of large mammals; has attacked man more than any other wild mammal has. Likes water and swims well; makes prodigious leaps; highly territorial habits. Endangered, chiefly by human destruction of its habitat. Of the eight subspecies known earlier this century, several are extinct or nearly so.

Wild cat (*Felis silvestris*). COLORATION: The European subspecies, depicted on this page, is yellow-gray, with pale belly, white throat, dark stripes on forehead and body, and rings and blackish tip on the tail. Length 30″, height 16″, weight 18 lb. The illustration on the facing page shows the African, Asian and Mediterranean subspecies *Felis silvestris libyca* (also known as African wild cat, Egyptian wild cat and Caffre cat; often considered a separate species, *Felis libyca*), which may be orange, sandy or gray with spots or stripes; length 28″, height 9″, weight 8 lb. (*More about wild cats on facing page.*)

Wild cat (continued). Lives in forested, grassy, open or rocky country over much of Eurasia from Britain into northern China, and in Africa. Probably the wild ancestor of the domestic cat. Solitary hunter, at night and dusk, of rodents and other small animals.